THIS LAND CALLED AMERICA: **TEXAS**

CREATIVE EDUCATION

Published by Creative Education
P.O. Box 227, Mankato, Minnesota 56002
Creative Education is an imprint of The Creative Company
www.thecreativecompany.us

Design by Blue Design (www.bluedes.com)
Art direction by Rita Marshall
Book production by The Design Lab
Printed in the United States of America

Photographs by Alamy (Stephen Bardens, H. Mark Weidman Photography,
Lebrecht Music and Arts Photo Library, North Wind Picture Archives), Corbis
(Bettmann, Nicole Fruge/San Antonio Express/ZUMA, Danny Gawlowski/
Dallas Morning News, Darrell Gulin, Stephanie Maze, David Muench, Jim
Sugar, Bo Zaunders), Dreamstime (Bowlingranny), Getty Images (William
Albert Allard/National Geographic, Michael Hart, Alan R. Moller, Paul
Spinelli, Texas Energy Museum/Newsmakers), iStockphoto (Linda Mirro,
January Smith)

Library of Congress Cataloging-in-Publication Data
Peterson, Sheryl.
Texas / by Sheryl Peterson.
p. cm. — (This land called America)
Includes bibliographical references and index.
ISBN 978-1-58341-796-6
1. Texas—Juvenile literature. I. Title. II. Series.
F386.3.P475 2009
976.4—dc22   2008009525

First Edition
9 8 7 6 5 4 3 2 1

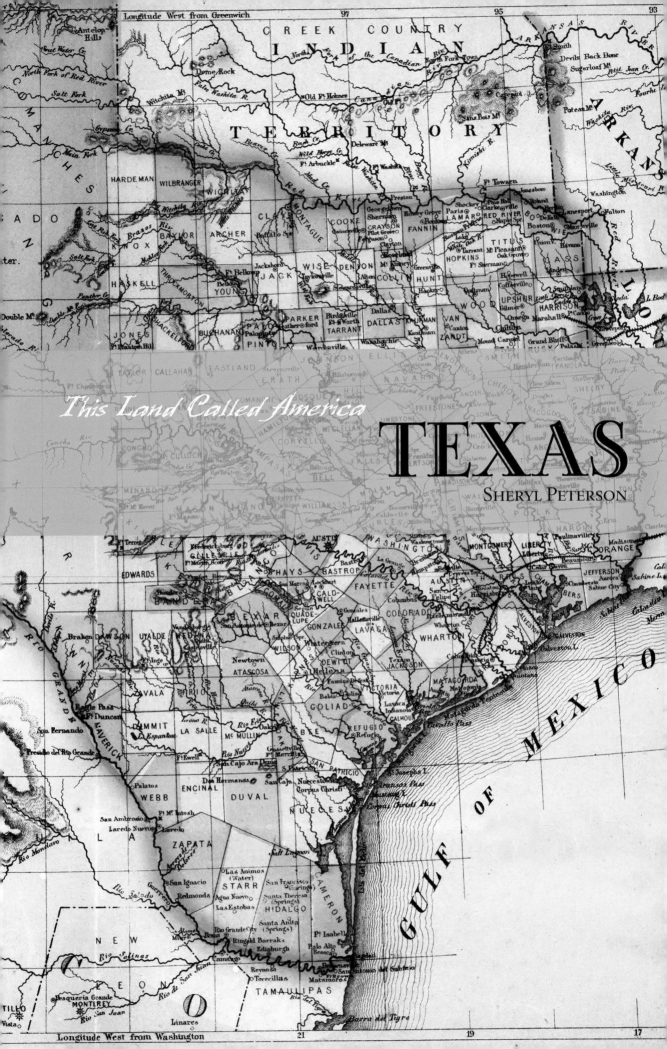

This Land Called America

TEXAS

Sheryl Peterson

Texas

SHERYL PETERSON

RIDE 'EM COWBOY! A RODEO RIDER STRUGGLES TO KEEP HIS BALANCE ON A BUCKING BRONCO. HE MUST STAY IN THE SADDLE FOR AT LEAST EIGHT SECONDS. TEXANS WHOOP AND HOLLER FROM THE STANDS, CHEERING HIM ON, AS HORSE HOOVES KICK UP CLOUDS OF DUST. TIME'S UP! THE RIDER LEAPS CLEAR OF HIS LIVE-WIRE HORSE AND WAVES HIS HAT AT THE CHEERING CROWD. NEARBY, COWBOYS AND COWGIRLS IN FLASHY SHIRTS WITH SILVER BUTTONS COMPETE IN BARREL RACING. OTHERS TRY THEIR LUCK AT TRICK RIDING. RODEOS OFFER SPILLS AND THRILLS FOR DARING RIDERS. TEXAS FANS CAN'T GET ENOUGH OF THE WILD, WESTERN FUN!

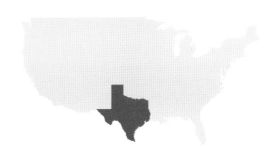

YEAR

1519 Alonso Álvarez de Piñeda sails into the Rio Grande and maps the Texas coastline.

EVENT

Six Flags State

Texans boast that six countries' or territories' flags have flown over the state's vast prairies, woods, and mountains. These flags include those of Spain, France, and Mexico. Spain first claimed what is now Texas in 1519. Alonso Álvarez de Piñeda was the first to map the area near the Gulf Coast. In 1528, another Spaniard named Alvar

Núñez Cabeza de Vaca explored the Texas wilderness. He found several native tribes there.

The Caddo tribe lived in farming villages. The Apache and Comanche Indians lived on the plains and were expert hunters. Puebloan tribes in western Texas grew corn and gathered the fruit of the prickly pear cactus. They built homes of adobe, or bricks made out of dried mud.

When Cabeza de Vaca crossed the dry land of Texas in the 1500s (opposite), he likely encountered Puebloan Indians in their adobe-built villages (above).

In 1685, French explorers moved into the area. French nobleman René-Robert de La Salle founded a colony on the Gulf Coast called Fort St. Louis. But disease, hostile Indians, and lack of food drove the Frenchmen out in only five years.

YEAR
| 1682 | The first Christian mission church is built at Ysleta in the mountains of western Texas. |

EVENT

State bird: mockingbird

By 1821, most of Texas was ruled by the newly independent Republic of Mexico. Stephen Austin, a Yale University-educated judge, led 300 American families to settle along the southern Brazos River in 1825. Many Texas families today can proudly trace their ties back to "The Old Three Hundred." Austin is remembered as "The Father of Texas."

The American settlers soon began to rebel against Mexican rule. On October 2, 1835, Texans, led by General Sam Houston, started the Texas Revolution and captured the city of San Antonio. Mexican leader Antonio López de Santa Anna sent 1,800 men to attack the Alamo, a former Spanish mission and American stronghold. The Alamo was defended by fewer than 200 Texans and was finally captured by Mexico after 13 days of fighting on March 6, 1836. Jim Bowie and Davy Crockett were among the brave men who died defending the Alamo. They became heroes in Texas folklore.

On April 21, 1836, Houston and his troops led a surprise attack against the Mexicans, winning the revolution and their freedom. Texas became an independent republic, with Houston serving as its first president.

On December 29, 1845, Texas became America's 28th state. Texas was nicknamed "The Lone Star State." Its state flag had only one star on it, as it did when Texas was a republic.

The Mexican army's victory at the Battle of the Alamo prompted many Texas colonists to immediately join Sam Houston's forces.

YEAR

1718   Mission San Antonio de Valero is founded and later becomes the city of San Antonio.

EVENT

However, Mexicans still thought Texas should be part of their country.

U.S. president James Polk sent diplomats to Mexico. But the neighboring countries could not agree on the land ownership. On May 13, 1846, the Mexican-American War began. After two years, Mexico surrendered and signed a treaty, or peace agreement. Mexico gave up nearly half of its territory, and a river named the Rio Grande became the Texas-Mexico boundary.

The 1860s and '70s marked the era of the long Texas cattle drives. People in the U.S. wanted beef, and thousands of longhorn cattle roamed freely on the Texas plains. Cowboys drove the cattle north to Montana to graze. Then the newly built railroads shipped the cattle across the country.

In 1901, Texas oil drillers hit a gusher. The Spindletop well near Beaumont spewed out crude oil called "black gold" for nine days. The Texas oil industry created new jobs, roads, and railroads all across the state. In the early 1900s, oil made Texas a wealthy place.

The longhorn cattle drives of the 1800s (above) and gushing oil wells such as the Spindletop (opposite) are iconic Texas images.

YEAR
1821   Texas becomes a state under the rule of the Republic of Mexico.
EVENT

- 10 -

Don't Fence Me In

TEXAS IS THE SECOND-LARGEST STATE, BEHIND ALASKA, IN TERMS OF LAND AREA. TEXAS LOOKS LIKE A ROUGH TRIANGLE. IT HAS A PANHANDLE JUTTING UP AT THE TOP. OKLAHOMA FORMS THE NORTHERN BORDER WITH TEXAS. LOUISIANA AND ARKANSAS ARE EASTERN NEIGHBORS. NEW MEXICO LIES TO THE WEST, AND MEXICO AND THE GULF OF MEXICO ARE TO THE SOUTH.

Within Big Bend National Park are the Grapevine Mountains, which feature unique rock formations.

There are mountains, seacoasts, and prairies in Texas. There are also desert lands and thick forests. The Piney Woods is a 750,000-acre (303,514 ha) belt of pine forests in eastern Texas. People travel there to fish in Lake Texoma on the Red River. It is the largest man-made lake or reservoir in the state. Big Thicket National Preserve covers thousands of acres of swamps, streams, and dense woods in this region. Caddo Lake, along the Louisiana border, is the only natural lake in Texas. Giant cypress trees draped with Spanish moss add charm to the lake. West Texas, in contrast, is hot, dry, and mountainous.

The Piney Woods region of East Texas includes longleaf pine (opposite) as well as shortleaf and loblolly pine trees.

Big Bend National Park is located where the Rio Grande makes a sharp bend. Rocky hills and steep canyons near the river provide homes for pronghorn, deer, and bighorn sheep. There are no cities for hundreds of miles. The flat, desert land is broken up by the rugged peaks of the Guadalupe, Davis, and Santiago mountains to the north of Big Bend.

YEAR

1822   The first American settlement in Texas, Austin's Colony, is established by adventurer Stephen Austin.

EVENT

Rolling prairies blanket the central plains of Texas, which is an area also known as the Texas Hill Country. The grassy plains provide plenty of good grazing land for cattle. Farmers grow wheat, corn, and hay there. Cotton is the top crop in the state.

The Texas coastal area stretches along the Gulf of Mexico. Saltwater marshes, bays, and islands lie off the coast. There are many fishing villages and busy ports. Shrimp boats cruise out to get the fresh catch of the day. Sandy beaches are sprinkled along the seashore. Orange, grapefruit, and palm trees grow in the nearby Rio Grande Valley. Houston, Texas's largest city, lies in this coastal region as well.

Although Texas cotton crops are today harvested using automated picking machines (above), fishing in the Gulf of Mexico continues to be a very hands-on process (opposite).

1861   Texas leaves the Union to join the Confederate States during the American Civil War.

EVENT

Bluebonnets, which are the state flower, are commonly seen along Texas roadsides in the springtime.

More than 5,000 species of wildflower bloom across central Texas. Goldenrods, Indian paintbrush, and bluebonnets are among the most common wildflowers. In eastern Texas, pine and oak trees stand tall, and in the west, mesquite trees, barrel cactus, and buffalo grasses dominate the landscape. Gulls, pelicans, egrets, and whooping cranes swoop along the winding eastern Texas coastline.

Texas has more deer than any other state. Rabbits, raccoons, and pronghorn are also at home in central Texas. Strange-looking armadillos and horned toads scurry over the dry land of West Texas. More than 100 kinds of snakes also slither around Texas. Fifteen of those, such as the western diamondback rattlesnake, are venomous.

Since Texas is so spread out, its climate varies greatly. In July, the average temperature is almost 96 °F (36 °C) statewide. Snow falls in the winter months in the north. The Panhandle has colder winters, while the Gulf Coast remains mild. Average rainfall is about 16 to 32 inches (41–81 cm). Texas's weather can be unpredictable and deadly. More tornadoes touch down in Texas than in any other state. Hurricanes that form in the Gulf of Mexico have a history of destruction. In 1900, a hurricane killed more than 8,000 people in the coastal city of Galveston and the surrounding area.

Texas weather can be unpredictable, but thunder and lightning are usually reliable signs that a storm is coming.

YEAR

1900   A hurricane destroys the city of Galveston and kills more than 8,000 people.

EVENT

Southern Neighbors

TEXANS ARE KNOWN FOR THEIR FRIENDLINESS. "HOWDY Y'ALL!" IS A GREETING THAT CAN BE HEARD ACROSS THE STATE. THE NAME TEXAS COMES FROM THE SPANISH SPELLING, *TEJAS*, OF A CADDO INDIAN WORD MEANING "FRIEND."

In the 1800s, European families first traveled to the wide-open spaces of eastern Texas. Germans were one of the largest immigrant groups. They settled around Houston, Galveston, and San Antonio. Irish, English, Danish, and Norwegian immigrants soon joined them.

Today, large cities such as Houston are good places for all Texas children to receive an education.

Today, Hispanics (of mostly Mexican ancestry) make up the biggest ethnic group in Texas. The state has close ties to Mexico, its Spanish-speaking neighbor to the south. Texas has a large African American population, along with many people of German, Norwegian, and Polish descent.

Many hard-working Texans have become well known. Jane Long was one of the first English-speaking women in Texas.

During Texas's frontier days, characters such as Judge Roy Bean (white-bearded man opposite) ruled their small towns.

YEAR

1910

EVENT

The first military air flight takes place at Fort Sam Houston, marking the beginning of the U.S. Air Force.

During World War II, Dwight Eisenhower (middle) worked with commanders of other countries' armies to achieve victory.

She was a member of Stephen Austin's first colony. Long bought and sold land, raised cattle, and grew cotton. Written on her tombstone are the words, "The Mother of Texas."

A more recent Texan whom many Americans respect is athlete Lance Armstrong. Armstrong was born in Plano. He won the Iron Kids Triathlon at age 13 and became a professional bicyclist. Armstrong wore the famous yellow winner's jersey seven times as champion of the Tour de France bicycle race.

Nolan Ryan is another Texas sports hero. Ryan was born in Refugio. The major league baseball pitcher was famous for pitching games in which no opposing batters could get a hit. Ryan played for the New York Mets, California Angels, Houston Astros, and Texas Rangers.

Two U.S. presidents were born in Texas. Dwight D. Eisenhower grew up in Denison. A popular general in World War II, Eisenhower became the 34th president. Lyndon B.

Lance Armstrong retired from competitive racing in 2005, but in 2008, he announced that he would return to the sport.

YEAR

1958 Texas Instruments develops the first silicon chip for use in electronic devices such as calculators.

EVENT

- *20* -

Johnson, also known as "LBJ," was the 36th president. His birth-place was Stonewall. Johnson was sworn into office after the 1963 shooting death of president John F. Kennedy in Dallas.

Johnson's wife, Claudia "Lady Bird" Johnson, grew up in Karnack, near the Louisiana border. She worked hard to beautify the Texas highways and save the native wildflowers. The Lyndon Baines Johnson Historical Park is in central Texas, near Johnson City. The park features an abundance of cheery wildflowers in the spring and summer.

Texas has one of the largest economies in the world. People in the state no longer just farm or raise cattle. Many work in the food processing business. Texas grain, beef, fruit, and veg-etables are shipped across the U.S. and to other countries.

People in Texas factories make airplanes and aerospace equipment. They also make parts for boats, cars, and trucks. Other Texans work in the oil industry. They pump oil out of the ground and work in plants that refine the oil into usable fuel.

Texas native Lyndon Johnson became president hours after John F. Kennedy was shot in Dallas.

At a petrochemical plant, oil can be refined to make chemicals that can be used in plastics and other products.

Cowboys still round up cattle in Texas. There are about 13 million cattle in the state. The most popular breeds are Hereford, Angus, and Santa Gertrudis. In 2005, there were more than 250,000 ranches and farms in Texas. Cattle ranching has shifted from the dry western area to the more humid eastern part of the state in recent years.

Farmers in Texas produce chili peppers, peanuts, and black-eyed peas. Watermelons, apples, and pears grow year-round in Texas. Most Christmas poinsettias and roses come from the state of Texas as well.

What's Big in Texas

There is an old saying in Texas: "All Texans have two hometowns: the one they live in and San Antonio." San Antonio is the heart and soul of Texas. The Alamo is its most popular tourist attraction. Not far away is the Institute of Texan Cultures, where people can learn about Texas history.

El Mercado is the Mexican market in San Antonio. It is a colorful collection of busy shops and restaurants. Tourists also visit the Mission San Jose. It is one of five old Spanish missions, or churches, still standing in the city. The city's famous River Walk winds along the San Antonio River. Paddleboats cruise on it, bright flowers bloom beside it, and tall pecan trees shade its banks.

Residents of San Antonio claim that chili was first made there in the 1800s. It is now the official state dish. There are chili cook-off contests all over Texas. True Texas chili has no beans, tomatoes, or bell peppers. It contains only hot chili peppers and beef. Texans' taste for spicy food was influenced by their Mexican neighbors. Restaurants across the U.S. now serve "Tex-Mex" dishes.

The Lyndon B. Johnson Space Center is located in southeast Houston. It is the home of the National Aeronautics and

San Antonio's five missions, including Mission San Jose (above), are all part of a national historical park today.

Restaurants along the San Antonio River Walk offer visitors waterside seating and a picturesque atmosphere.

YEAR

1973 Houston's Manned Spacecraft Center is renamed the Lyndon B. Johnson Space Center.

EVENT

The Dallas Cowboys have won 5 Super Bowls and 10 conference championships since joining the NFL in 1960.

Space Administration (NASA). NASA is the leading center for space exploration in the U.S. NASA launched the Saturn V rocket that sent the Apollo 11 mission to the moon. It also created the space shuttle that carried the Spacelab far out into space. At the "Kids' Space Place," kids can climb inside a space shuttle and experience what life on a space station is like.

Texans are passionate about their sports. Football fever starts young with high school rivalries and expands to powerful college teams. Texans also cheer for the Dallas Cowboys or the Houston Texans, both professional football teams. In 2009, the Cowboys moved from Irving, Texas, to a new multimillion-dollar stadium with a retractable roof in Arlington.

Texas baseball fans follow two professional teams, the Houston Astros and the Texas Rangers. A pro hockey team, the Dallas Stars, takes center ice at the American Airlines Center in Dallas. For exciting professional basketball action, fans turn to the Houston Rockets, Dallas Mavericks, and San Antonio Spurs.

NASA astronauts in training can experience what weightlessness in space feels like by using simulators.

YEAR
2003 On February 1, the space shuttle *Columbia* disintegrates over Texas during re-entry into Earth's atmosphere.
EVENT

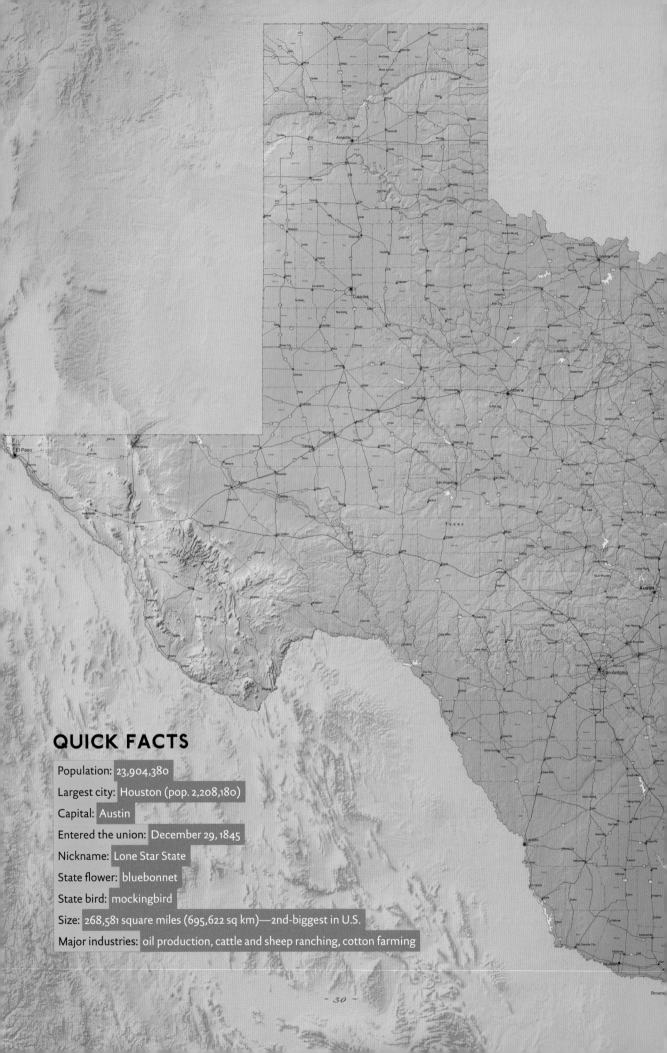

QUICK FACTS

Population: 23,904,380

Largest city: Houston (pop. 2,208,180)

Capital: Austin

Entered the union: December 29, 1845

Nickname: Lone Star State

State flower: bluebonnet

State bird: mockingbird

Size: 268,581 square miles (695,622 sq km)—2nd-biggest in U.S.

Major industries: oil production, cattle and sheep ranching, cotton farming

People enjoy the outdoors in the warm weather of Texas. The Gulf Coast of Texas remains a favorite place for vacationers. Padre Island, known for its pearly white sand, sweeps in a southward arc for 113 miles (182 km) from Corpus Christi to just north of the Mexican border. Visitors from northern states flock down to the island to escape cold winters. Some people charter boats to try deep-sea fishing. Others jet ski or go parasailing. Lucky fishermen come home with catches of sailfish, marlin, and red snapper. Swimmers enjoy the bath-warm waters and sandy beaches.

Texas is more than what people see in old Western movies. There are thousands of square miles of rolling prairies where cowboys still ride the range. At the same time, skyscrapers also rise up from modern cities. With its rugged mountains, thick pine forests, and sunny Gulf coastline, the Lone Star State is a place that Texans are hugely proud of and that other people can't wait to visit.

BIBLIOGRAPHY

Anderson, Adrian. *Texas and Texans*. New York: McGraw-Hill/Glencoe, 2003.

Campbell, Randolph. *Gone to Texas*. Oxford: Oxford University Press, 2003.

Galit, Elaine, and Vikk Simmons. *Exploring Texas History*. Lanham, Md.: Taylor Trade Publishing, 2005.

Sasek, Miroslav. *This Is Texas*. New York: Universe, 2006.

Travel Texas. "Homepage." Office of the Governor, Economic Development and Tourism. http://www.traveltex.com.

INDEX